GreenScape Granbury LLC

I0012068

HOW TO BUILD A WEBSITE USING HTML, PHP, AND MYSQL

AUTHOR

WES SENTER

GreenScape Granbury LLC

COPYRIGHT © 2023 WES SENTER
All rights reserved.

GreenScape Granbury LLC

Contents

Chapter 1: Overview

Most of the information that you require is included in this manual and is just a few clicks away!

To save time in the future, print a copy of this document. Choose Print from the File menu, and press Enter to receive all pages of examples and instructions. With the printed document in hand, you are ready to begin the process of learning how to build your web site and manage it for yourself or paying customers.

Introduction

Welcome and thank you for purchasing a copy of my eBook. This manual was created as an effort to inform and guide the reader in the operational and technical aspects of creating websites using HTML, PHP and MySQL. Once you have read this manual, you should have a good understanding of the "what" and "how" of this material. My name is Wes Senter. I am a Computer Scientist and have been working in this field for over thirty-five years.

About Greenscape Granbury LLC

This document was designed and written with the layman in mind. This manual is very intuitive and simplified for a beginner. I do not go into detail in this document. I designed this book so the reader can copy and paste working html, css, and scripts while you follow along with this manual.

Overview of the Book's Content
We will begin by covering the basics of HTML, PHP and MySQL

HTML or Hypertext Markup Language is the language that most websites are developed with. It is used to form the structure of the website.

PHP stands for Hypertext Preprocessor. It is an open-source, server-side, HTML embedded scripting language. Its strength lies in its compatibility with many types of databases.

MySQL is an open-source relational database management system. It is also a Structured Query Language used to access databases.

CSS is an abbreviation for Cascading Style Sheets. It is a style sheet language, used to construct the presentation of an HTML web page.

Using this eBook, we are going to create a website using the four languages listed above. We will illustrate how PHP integrates with HTML to both secure website pages and read, write, and delete data from a MySQL database.

We will first create an index.php file and start there. Why index.php? Because Apache looks for index.html or index.php as the default start-up file.

About Domain Names and Name Servers
Every website requires a domain name. Our website is "greenscapellc.com" and it is registered at GoDaddy. If you wish to build a website and give it a domain name, you will need a web server to run it on.

Many companies will lease you a "VPS". This stands for "Virtual Private Server". A VPS is a space that has been carved out of a large server with a lot of memory. Several VPSs typically run on one server. A VPS is where you will upload your website. At this point, we get into web servers which are not covered in this book. I

have written another eBook named "How to Build Your Own Web Server". It is available on Kindle. It has the same style of book cover.

You may have thought, how can someone in New York pull up my website over the internet. The answer to that question is because of "Name Servers". These servers do several things. First, they route data packets from one Name Server to the next. They also calculate the shortest path between the sender and the receiver. This is accomplished by utilizing routing protocols such as BGP. Now that I have really confused you, let's talk about the programming side of things.

Pre-Requisites

You will need several things to perform this lesson. They are listed below.

1. Space on a web server to be able to copy your web pages into.

2. A good PHP editor, if you have it. I prefer "Microsoft VSC". It is Free and one of the best IDEs (Integrated Development Environments). It is much more than an editor. If you prefer a simpler PHP editor, download Notepad ++. It is also free.

3. FTP or File Transfer Protocol. Many people use "FileZilla". It is free. You will use this to upload your webpages to your web server. We will not be using it for this lesson. There is no need, as we will be working directly in your www folder.

4. MySQL and PHP are most likely already installed on your server when you lease one.

If you do not have access to a web server with PHP and MySQL, no problem. There is an alternative to use until you can get a real server. See Chapter 2.

Chapter 2: Getting Started with AMPPS

AMPPS basically turns your Windows 10 or 11 PC into a Linux Server. It comes loaded with PHP and MySQL. You will not lose any Windows functionality on your existing computer. We will download and install this so you can build your website on your local computer!

Installing AMPPS on Windows 10 or 11

Go to http://ampps.com and click the button to download, on the website's home page. You will have to join their membership (No cost). Then download the exe file and install it. You may be prompted to install Microsoft C++. If you see this prompt, be sure to install it. AMPPS will do this for you.

Reboot your computer. When it is running again, click the Ampps icon on your desktop. Click the globe icon on the Ampps box and you should have a popup browser with the beginnings of a new website. If this worked ok, click the house icon on the Ampps window. You should now see a new browser for Ampps. Once you are on the Ampps main control panel, create a bookmark for this page.

By default, AMPPS will use the following location on your drive as the document root:

C:\Program Files\Ampps\www.

Once you start saving your HTML files into this directory, you will run the website by entering "http://localhost" into your browser.

To ensure that everything is working the way it should, let's create a basic website and run it.

1. Using your editor of choice, copy and paste the following HTML code into your editor:

```
<!DOCTYPE html>
<html lang="en">
  <head>
```

GreenScape Granbury LLC

```
  <title>How to Build Your Own Website</title>
 </head>
 <body>
   How to Build Your Own Web Server | Available on Kindle.
 </body>
</html>
```

2. Save the above to C:\Program Files\Ampps\www\test.html.
3. Now, in your browser enter "localhost/test.html to run the program.
4. From now on, you can copy your files to the /www directory to hold your website and your website will run on your computer using Ampps!

Chapter 3: Including PHP with HTML

Most of the information that you require is included in this manual and is just a few clicks away!

By default, PHP documents end with the extension *.php*. PHP code begins with *<?php* and ends with *?>* .

Now, let's create a small php program and test it using the same directory as we tested the HTML program. Bring up your editor and enter this php script.

```
<?php
   echo "How to Build Your Own Web Server";
?>
```

1. Save the above to C:\Program Files\Ampps\www\test.php
2. Now, in your browser enter "localhost/test.php to run the program.

An Overview of Forms

Forms are very common when building a website. They are written in HTML and require <form> <input statements></form> tags. This "< div >" is a tag with an HTML statement inside it.

Let's build a login form to see how it works. Copy and paste the following code into a new file called login.php below. Start with <?php and end the copy with ?>.

The top half of this file is PHP. The second half is HTML (mostly). I have added remarks out to the right of each command line to explain what is going on.

```
<?php                    //Start PHP
   session_start();      //Required to allow PHP to be able to pick-up the SESSION
command later on.

   include ('config.php');        //Include the Database connectivity information file.

   error_reporting(E_ALL);        //Turns on error reporting
   ini_set("display_errors", 1);

if (isset ($_POST['username']) && !empty ($_POST['username'])  //If username is
posted continue
         && !empty ($_POST['password'])) {


$user = $_POST['username'];          //form value username is taken from post.
Assigned to $user.
$pass = $_POST['password'];            //Same as the above but for password.
// MySQL query to select all records from the users table where username matches
$user/$pass
```

```php
$result=mysqli_query($db,"select * from users where username='$user' AND
password='$pass'");

if (!$result) {                  //If not result is true process all commands up to the "}".
                echo '<div><p>Error Accessing Database<br />
                        Error: . mysqli_error() . "</p>" .
                    "<p>" . Click to Return to the Login Page. <a href="login.php">Click
Here</a></div>';
            }

//check that at least one row was returned
$rowCheck = mysqli_num_rows($result);        //Set the number of rows that were
returned
if($rowCheck > 0){                               //Is the number greater than 0?
while($row = mysqli_fetch_array($result)){    //If so, get the records into the $result
array

  //start the session and register a variable
  $_SESSION['username'] = $user;         //This is why we used session_start above

  header( "Location: index.php" );        //Direct you to index.php
  }
}                                  //And, Close
else {
//if nothing is returned by the query, unsuccessful login code goes here...
?>

  <script type="text/javascript">
  alert("ERROR! Wrong Login ID or Password!");        //Else run this JavaScript code
  </script>

<?php
 }
 }
 ?>
```

```html
<!DOCTYPE html>
<html lang="en">
 <head>
  <meta charset="UTF-8">
  <meta name="viewport" content="width=device-width, initial-scale=1.0">
  <title>Registration or Sign Up</title>
  <link rel="stylesheet" href="stylelr.css">
 </head>
<body>
 <div class="wrapper">
  <h2>Sign In To System</h2>
  <form action="<?php echo $_SERVER['PHP_SELF']; ?>" method="post">
   <div class="input-box">
    <input type="text" name="username" placeholder="Enter your username"
required>
   </div>
   <div class="input-box">
    <input type="password" name="password" placeholder="Enter your password"
required>
   </div>
   <div class="policy">
    <input type="checkbox">
    <h3>I accept all terms & condition</h3>
   </div>
   <div class="input-box button">
    <input type="Submit" value="Login">
   </div>
   <div class="text">
    <h3>Don't have an account? <a href="register.php"> Register
now</a></h3>
   </div>
  </form>
 </div>
</body>
```

GreenScape Granbury LLC

```html
</html>
```

File Name: login.php (Create this file in the C:\Program Files\Ampps\www directory).

```php
// ----------------------------- Start Copy at <?php

<?php
session_start();

include ('config.php');

error_reporting(E_ALL);

ini_set("display_errors", 1);

//---------------------------------------------------------------------------------------

//

$db = mysqli_connect("$dbHost", "$dbUser", "$dbPass", "$dbDatabase");

if (isset ($_POST['username']) && !empty ($_POST['username'])
&& !empty ($_POST['password'])) {

//convert the field values to simple variables

$user = $_POST['username'];
$pass = $_POST['password'];

$result=mysqli_query($db,"select * from users where username='$user' AND
password='$pass'");
```

```php
if (!$result) {
echo '<div><p>Error Accessing Database<br />

Error: . mysqli_error() . "</p>" .
"<p>" . Click to Return to the Login Page . <a href="login.php">Click Here</a></div>';
}

//check that at least one row was returned

$rowCheck = mysqli_num_rows($result);
if($rowCheck > 0){

while($row = mysqli_fetch_array($result)){

//start the session and register a variable

$_SESSION['username'] = $user;



//successful login code will go here...
//we will redirect the user to another page where we will make sure they're logged in

header( "Location: index.php" );

}

} else {

  //if nothing is returned by the query, unsuccessful login code goes here...

?>      //Turn off PHP so we can run JavaScript

<script type="text/javascript">
alert("ERROR! Wrong Login ID or Password!");
</script>
```

GreenScape Granbury LLC

```php
<?php            // Turn PHP back on

}
}
?>               //End PHP – Start HTML Section Below
```

```html
<!DOCTYPE html>
<html lang="en">

<head>
<meta charset="UTF-8">
<meta name="viewport" content="width=device-width, initial-scale=1.0">
<title>Registration or Sign Up</title>
<link rel="stylesheet" href="stylelr.css">
</head>

<body>
<div class="wrapper">
<h2>Sign In To System</h2>

<form action="<?php echo $_SERVER['PHP_SELF']; ?>" method="post">

<div class="input-box">
<input type="text" name="username" placeholder="Enter your username" required>
</div>

<div class="input-box">

 <input type="password" name="password" placeholder="Enter your password"
required>
 </div>

 <div class="policy">
```

GreenScape Granbury LLC

```html
<input type="checkbox">
<h3>I accept all terms & condition</h3>
</div>

<div class="input-box button">
<input type="Submit" value="Login">
</div>

<div class="text">
<h3>Don't have an account? <a href="insert.php"> Register now</a></h3>
</div>

</form>
</div>
</body>
</html>
```

// ----------------------------- End Copy at </html> above.

Taking a Closer Look at Login.php

Starting at the top of the script, on the third line, you will see:

include ('config.php')

The include statement finds the file named **config.php** and loads it into login.php when the login file is executed. The config file that you are about to create contains the database connectivity information. This statement is entirely optional. You could put the database definitions in login.php. However, it is a good idea to separate commonly used code and place it in its own file. This makes for a smaller script, and it is more efficient.

Create the config.php file.

GreenScape Granbury LLC

Create the file, named "config.php". If you scroll up and look in the source code of login.php, you will see this in the header. Save it in the same directory as the login.php file. This script allows your login.php file to connect to your database. Copy and paste the code below into **config.php**. Be certain that the values in the config.php file match what you entered in the MySQL database. That is coming up soon. This will include the database name, the database username/privileges, and the user's password. Do not change "localhost".

config.php source code. (Create this file in the C:\Program Files\Ampps\www directory).

```php
<?

// Hostname of your database server
$dbHost='localhost';

// Your database username
$dbUser='gs995';

// Your database password
$dbPass='gsp9075';

// The name of the database that AHD will use
$dbDatabase='greenscape';

$db = mysqli_connect("$dbHost", "$dbUser", "$dbPass", "$dbDatabase");

if (!$db)
{
echo "Failed to connect to MySQL: " . mysqli_connect_error();
}

mysqli_select_db($db, "greenscape");

?
```

Create the stylelr.css file.

GreenScape Granbury LLC

You will also need the stylelr.css file to properly format your login.php page. The pointer to your .css file is found in the HTML Header of the login.php script and looks like this:

```
<link rel="stylesheet" href="stylelr.css">
```

Create a new file in the C: \Program Files\Ampps\www directory called "stylelr.css". Open your editor and copy the css code below and paste it into your editor. Save the file and Name it "stylelr.css".

stylelr.css source code. (Create this file in the C:\Program Files\Ampps\www directory).

```
@import
url('https://fonts.googleapis.com/css?family=Poppins:400,500,600,700&display=swap'
);

*{

margin: 0;
padding: 0;
box-sizing: border-box;
font-family: 'Poppins', sans-serif;
}

body{
min-height: 100vh;
display: flex;
align-items: center;
justify-content: center;
background: #4070f4;
}
.wrapper{
position: relative;
max-width: 430px;
```

GreenScape Granbury LLC

```css
width: 100%;
background: #fff;
padding: 34px;

border-radius: 6px;
box-shadow: 0 5px 10px rgba(0,0,0,0.2);
}
.wrapper h2{
position: relative;
font-size: 22px;
font-weight: 600;
color: #333;
}
.wrapper h2::before{
content: "
position: absolute;
left: 0;
bottom: 0;
height: 3px;
width: 28px;
border-radius: 12px;
background: #4070f4;
}
.wrapper form{
margin-top: 30px;
}
.wrapper form .input-box{
height: 52px;
margin: 18px 0;
}
form .input-box input{
height: 100%;
width: 100%;
outline: none;
padding: 0 15px;
```

```
font-size: 17px;
font-weight: 400;
color: #333;
border: 1.5px solid #C7BEBE;
border-bottom-width: 2.5px;
border-radius: 6px;
transition: all 0.3s ease;
}
.input-box input:focus,
.input-box input:valid{

border-color: #4070f4;
}
form .policy{
display: flex;
align-items: center;
}
form h3{
color: #707070;
font-size: 14px
font-weight: 500;
margin-left: 10px;
}
.input-box.button input{
color: #fff;
letter-spacing: 1px;
border: none;
background: #4070f4;
cursor: pointer;
}
.input-box.button input:hover{
background: #0e4bf1;
}
form .text h3{
color: #333;
```

```
width: 100%;
text-align: center;
}
form .text h3 a{
color: #4070f4;
text-decoration: none;
}
form .text h3 a:hover{
text-decoration: underline;
}
```

Now, Create the style.css file.

You will also need the style.css file to properly format the rest of your pages. The pointer to your .css file is found in the HTML Header of the rest of the pages and looks like this:

```
<link rel="stylesheet" href="style.css">
```

Create a new file in the C: \Program Files\Ampps\www directory called "style.css".
Open your editor and copy the css code below and paste it into your editor.
Save the file and Name it "style.css".

style.css source code. (Create this file in the C:\Program Files\Ampps\www directory).

```
@import
url('https://fonts.googleapis.com/css?family=Poppins:400,500,600,700&display=swap'
);

*{
margin: 0;
```

```
padding: 0;
box-sizing: border-box;
font-family: 'Poppins', sans-serif;
}
body{
min-height: 100vh;
display: flex;
align-items: center
justify-content: center;
background: #4070f4;
}
.sidebar{
position: fixed;
height: 100%
width: 240px;
background: #0A2558;
transition: all 0.5s ease;
}
.sidebar.active{
width: 60px;
}
.sidebar .logo-details{
height: 80px;
display: flex;
align-items: center;
}
.sidebar .logo-details i{
font-size: 28px;
font-weight: 500;
color: #fff;
min-width: 60px;
text-align: center
}
.sidebar .logo-details .logo_name{
color: #fff;
```

```
font-size: 24px;
font-weight: 500;
}
.sidebar .nav-links{
margin-top: 10px;
}
.sidebar .nav-links li{
position: relative;
list-style: none;
height: 50px;
}
.sidebar .nav-links li a{
height: 100%;
width: 100%;
display: flex;
align-items: center;
text-decoration: none;
transition: all 0.4s ease;
}
.sidebar .nav-links li a.active{
background: #081D45;
}
.sidebar .nav-links li a:hover{
background: #081D45;
}
.sidebar .nav-links li i{
min-width: 60px;
text-align: center;
font-size: 18px;
color: #fff;
}
.sidebar .nav-links li a .links_name{
color: #fff;
font-size: 15px;
font-weight: 400;
```

GreenScape Granbury LLC

```
white-space: nowrap;
}
.sidebar .nav-links .log_out{
position: absolute;
bottom: 0;
width: 100%;
}
.home-section{
position: relative;
background: #f5f5f5;
min-height: 100vh;
width: calc(100% - 240px);
left: 240px;
transition: all 0.5s ease;
}
.sidebar.active ~ .home-section{
width: calc(100% - 60px);
left: 60px;
}
.home-section nav{
display: flex;
justify-content: space-between;
height: 80px;
background: #fff;
display: flex;
align-items: center
position: fixed;
width: calc(100% - 240px);
left: 240px;
z-index: 100;
padding: 0 20px;
box-shadow: 0 1px 1px rgba(0, 0, 0, 0.1);
transition: all 0.5s ease;
}
.sidebar.active ~ .home-section nav{
```

GreenScape Granbury LLC

```css
left: 60px
width: calc(100% - 60px);
}
.home-section nav .sidebar-button{
display: flex
align-items: center;
font-size: 24px;
font-weight: 500;
}
nav .sidebar-button i{
font-size: 35px;
margin-right: 10px;
}
.home-section nav .search-box{
position: relative;
height: 50px;
max-width: 550px;
width: 100%;
margin: 0 20px;
}
nav .search-box input{
height: 100%;
width: 100%;
outline: none;
background: #F5F6FA
border: 2px solid #EFEEF1;
border-radius: 6px;
font-size: 18px;
padding: 0 15px;
}
nav .search-box .bx-search{
position: absolute;
height: 40px;
width: 40px;
background: #2697FF;
```

```
right: 5px;
top: 50%;
transform: translateY(-50%);
border-radius: 4px;
line-height: 40px;
text-align: center;
color: #fff;
font-size: 22px;
transition: all 0.4 ease;
}
.home-section nav .profile-details{
display: flex
align-items: center;
background: #F5F6FA;
border: 2px solid #EFEEF1;
border-radius: 6px;
height: 50px;
min-width: 190px;
padding: 0 15px 0 2px;
}
nav .profile-details img{
height: 40px;
width: 40px;
border-radius: 6px;
object-fit: cover;
}
nav .profile-details .admin_name{
font-size: 15px;
font-weight: 500;
color: #333;
margin: 0 10px;
white-space: nowrap;
}
nav .profile-details i{
  font-size: 25px;
```

GreenScape Granbury LLC

```
  color: #333;
}
.home-section .home-content{
  position: relative;
  padding-top: 104px;
}
.home-content .overview-boxes{
  display: flex;
  align-items: center;
  justify-content: space-between;
  flex-wrap: wrap;
  padding: 0 20px;
  margin-bottom: 26px;
}
.overview-boxes .box{
  display: flex;
  align-items: center;
  justify-content: center;
  width: calc(100% / 4 - 15px);
  background: #fff;
  padding: 15px 14px;
  border-radius: 12px;
  box-shadow: 0 5px 10px rgba(0,0,0,0.1);
}
.overview-boxes .box-topic{
  font-size: 20px;
  font-weight: 500;
}
.home-content .box .number{
  display: inline-block;
  font-size: 35px;
  margin-top: -6px;
  font-weight: 500;
}
.home-content .box .indicator{
```

```
 display: flex;
 align-items: center;
}
.home-content .box .indicator i{
 height: 20px;
 width: 20px;
 background: #8FDACB;
 line-height: 20px;
 text-align: center;
 border-radius: 50%;
 color: #fff;
 font-size: 20px;
 margin-right: 5px;
}
.box .indicator i.down{
 background: #e87d88;
}
.home-content .box .indicator .text{
 font-size: 12px;
}
.home-content .box .cart{
 display: inline-block;
 font-size: 32px;
 height: 50px;
 width: 50px;
 background: #cce5ff;
 line-height: 50px;
 text-align: center;
 color: #66b0ff;
 border-radius: 12px;
 margin: -15px 0 0 6px;
}
.home-content .box .cart.two{
  color: #2BD47D;
  background: #C0F2D8;
```

```
 }
.home-content .box .cart.three{
  color: #ffc233;
  background: #ffe8b3;
 }
.home-content .box .cart.four{
  color: #e05260;
  background: #f7d4d7;
 }
.home-content .total-order{
  font-size: 20px;
  font-weight: 500;
}
.home-content .sales-boxes{
  display: flex;
  justify-content: space-between;
  /* padding: 0 20px; */
}
/* left box */
.home-content .sales-boxes .recent-sales{
  width: 65%;
  background: #fff;
  padding: 20px 30px;
  margin: 0 20px;
  border-radius: 12px;
  box-shadow: 0 5px 10px rgba(0, 0, 0, 0.1);
}
.home-content .sales-boxes .sales-details{
  display: flex;
  align-items: center;
  justify-content: space-between;
}
.sales-boxes .box .title{
  font-size: 24px;
  font-weight: 500;
```

```css
  /* margin-bottom: 10px; */
}
.sales-boxes .sales-details li.topic{
  font-size: 20px;
  font-weight: 500;
}
.sales-boxes .sales-details li{
  list-style: none;
  margin: 8px 0;
}
.sales-boxes .sales-details li a{
  font-size: 18px;
  color: #333;
  font-size: 400;
  text-decoration: none;
}
.sales-boxes .box .button{
  width: 100%;
  display: flex;
  justify-content: flex-end;
}
.sales-boxes .box .button a{
  color: #fff;
  background: #0A2558;
  padding: 4px 12px;
  font-size: 15px;
  font-weight: 400;
  border-radius: 4px;
  text-decoration: none;
  transition: all 0.3s ease;
}
.sales-boxes .box .button a:hover{
  background: #0d3073;
}
/* Right box */
```

GreenScape Granbury LLC

```css
.home-content .sales-boxes .top-sales{
  width: 35%;
  background: #fff;
  padding: 20px 30px;
  margin: 0 20px 0 0;
  border-radius: 12px;
  box-shadow: 0 5px 10px rgba(0, 0, 0, 0.1);
}
.sales-boxes .top-sales li{
  display: flex;
  align-items: center;
  justify-content: space-between;
  margin: 10px 0;
}
.sales-boxes .top-sales li a img{
  height: 40px;
  width: 40px;
  object-fit: cover;
  border-radius: 12px;
  margin-right: 10px;
  background: #333;
}
.sales-boxes .top-sales li a{
  display: flex;
  align-items: center;
  text-decoration: none;
}
.sales-boxes .top-sales li .product,
.price{
  font-size: 17px;
  font-weight: 400;
  color: #333;
}
/* Responsive Media Query */
@media (max-width: 1240px) {
```

GreenScape Granbury LLC

```
  .sidebar{
   width: 60px;
  }
  .sidebar.active{
   width: 220px;
  }
  .home-section{
   width: calc(100% - 60px);
   left: 60px;
  }
  .sidebar.active ~ .home-section{
   /* width: calc(100% - 220px); */
   overflow: hidden;
   left: 220px;
  }
  .home-section nav{
   width: calc(100% - 60px);
   left: 60px;
  }
  .sidebar.active ~ .home-section nav{
   width: calc(100% - 220px);
   left: 220px;
  }
}
@media (max-width: 1150px) {
 .home-content .sales-boxes{
   flex-direction: column;
  }
 .home-content .sales-boxes .box{
   width: 100%;
   overflow-x: scroll;
   margin-bottom: 30px;
  }
 .home-content .sales-boxes .top-sales{
   margin: 0;
```

```
 }
}
@media (max-width: 1000px) {
 .overview-boxes .box{
  width: calc(100% / 2 - 15px);
  margin-bottom: 15px;
 }
}
@media (max-width: 700px) {
 nav .sidebar-button .dashboard,
 nav .profile-details .admin_name,
 nav .profile-details i{
  display: none;
 }
 .home-section nav .profile-details{
  height: 50px;
  min-width: 40px;
 }
 .home-content .sales-boxes .sales-details{
  width: 560px;
 }
}
@media (max-width: 550px) {
 .overview-boxes .box{
  width: 100%;
  margin-bottom: 15px;
 }
 .sidebar.active ~ .home-section nav .profile-details{
  display: none;
 }
}
 @media (max-width: 400px) {
 .sidebar{
  width: 0;
 }
```

```
.sidebar.active{
 width: 60px;
}
.home-section{
 width: 100%;
 left: 0;
}
.sidebar.active ~ .home-section{
 left: 60px;
 width: calc(100% - 60px);
}
.home-section nav{
 width: 100%;
 left: 0;
}
.sidebar.active ~ .home-section nav{
 left: 60px;
 width: calc(100% - 60px);
 }
}
```

It's Time to Recap What We Have Accomplished

At this point, we need to check our work. There are always bugs to fix. Here is what we have done to this point.

1. We created the Login.php file.
2. We created the Config.php file.
3. We created the stylelr.css file.
4. We created the style.css file.

Next, we will create the database and populate one record containing the username and password.

Time To Create the Database

You have completed the config.php file and saved it in 'C:\Program Files\Ampps\www. Once again, this file contains the connection to your database. To create the database, follow the steps below.

5. On the Ampps popup window, click the house icon.
6. Under Database Tools, click phpMyAdmin.
7. The login to phpMyAdmin is "root" and the default password is "mysql".
8. In the left column, click "New".
9. Enter the Database Name. Let's call it "greenscape". Click the Create button.
10. Now, you should be on the "Create new table" panel.
11. Enter "users" in the Table Name field. Change "4" to "6" in the number of columns. Click the Create button.
12. Now, we will define each column, entering name, type, length, and index.
13. Starting with the topmost column name, enter the following, working your way down.
14. Name(uid), Type (INT), Check the A_I box.
15. Name(first), Type (VARCHAR), Length (50)
16. Name(last), Type (VARCHAR), Length (50)
17. Name(username), Type (VARCHAR), Length (50)
18. Name(password), Type (VARCHAR), Length (50)
19. Name(email), Type (VARCHAR), Length (100)
20. Click "Save" at the bottom of the panel.

Now, we will need to add a user with full privileges to the database. This is the username that is used in the config.php file for accessing the database. Don't confuse this with the username that is used to login. That will come later.

1. Click the "Privileges TAB".
2. Click "Add user account". For Username, enter "green100".
3. For Password, enter "Green509".

4. Under Global privileges, click the "Check All box".
5. Click "Go" at the bottom of the panel.

Don't change the database name, table name, or user information. These values are already coded into the config.php file and they must match.

Seeding the Database

Before running the program, you just created, we must add a user to the user's table. Currently, if you run login.php, there are no database records to search for. Follow the steps below.

1. Double click the Ampps icon on your computer's screen.
2. Click the house icon of the Ampps popup window.
3. Click the phpMyAdmin icon under Database Tools
4. Login to phpMyAdmin. User ID is "root". The default password is "mysql".
5. Click the "greenscape" database in the left column.
6. To the right of the users table, click Insert.
7. At the top, in the first empty field, column uid, skip this field. We set it earlier to "autoincrement".
8. In the "first" column, enter your first name. Enter it in the right-side field under the Value column.
9. In the "last" column, enter your last name. Enter it in the right-side field under the Value column.
10. In the "username" column, enter your username. Keep it simple and write it down.
11. In the "password" column, enter your password. The same as above.
12. Click the "Go" button that is under the fields and to the right.
13. On the new page, click the "Go" button again.
14. You should now see "1 row inserted".
15. Click "Browse" in the top menu to see the record you just inserted.

GreenScape Granbury LLC

Now, It Is Test Time.

Before we can move on, we need to test what we have built so far. Follow the steps below.

1. If you are not already in the C:\Program Files\Ampps\www directory, go to it.
2. Run your browser, preferably "Google Chrome". Enter "localhost/login.php".
3. If you coded everything properly, you should see the panel shown below.

Try to login using the username and password you created in the user's table. If your login is not showing up, go back and double check everything.

If the login panel does not appear, check the following.

1. Did you receive an error code of some type?
2. Common issues are Database Connectivity.
3. Compare the config.php values to the database values. Database name, Username, Password, and Privileges can all be checked in PhpMyAdmin. Run it from the Ampp popup window.
4. Are your username and password valid. An error message showing that problem will pop up, telling you. That is why it is important to write your IDs down.

5. If the panel shown on the previous page does not look the same, it will be a .css file problem. Go back and check that you copied all the .css code into stylelr.css and the file is in the root directory.
6. Assuming everything is good at this point, we will continue to the next section.
7. If you are just plain stuck and can't figure out what the problem is, email me at support@greenscapellc.com .

Using PHP to Secure Web Pages

If you want to offer secure login credentials to clients, PHP and MySQL work well. You can protect as many web pages as you want. You have to login using a valid Username and Password to access protected pages. Otherwise, you can't access the page(s).

This is accomplished by building a php script that checks whether you are logged in or not. You get the login values and do some checking using php. Then you use php again to read the required fields in the users table in MySQL. You then set a SESSION variable to store the login value and then use that value prior to loading any page to see if the SESSION value is valid. Let's create the code. The call to the script shown below goes at the very top of any page you wish to protect. Create "checkLogin.php". Copy and paste the following code into it.

```php
<?php

//start the session
session_start();

//check to make sure the session variable is registered

if (!isset($_SESSION[$user])) {

//if the session variable isn't registered, send them back to the login page. The session
variable is set at login. You can see this in the "login.php" file, $_SESSION['username'] =
```

GreenScape Granbury LLC

$user;.

header("Location: login.php");
}

?>

The 4th line above shows:

```
if (!isset($_SESSION[$user])) {
```

The above statement says, If the $user session is not set, execute the next statement(s) within the braces which is a redirect to login.php. Otherwise, continue. The exclamation point in front of the "isset" statement means NOT.

If a user has not signed in, the Session Variable has not been set. So, the script will execute the next statement within the braces which is header("Location: login.php");. This statement means to exit this script and redirect to "login.php" where the person trying to login sees the login form. He is back to where he started.

Create a new file called "checkLogin.php" in the www directory. Copy the above code starting with <?php and ending with ?>. Paste it into the new file and save it.

Then, on pages you want to protect, enter "include ('checkLogin.php');" at the very top of the page.

Be careful which pages you put this script on. Do not put this on your login.php or register.php forms. The reason why is obvious.

Let's Build a Website

Now that we have completed the required php script files, we can start building our website. Listed below are the php files you should have in your /web directory.

1. config.php
2. checkLogin.php
3. style.css
4. stylelr.css
5. login.php

The Index File

This is the default page for this website. You will notice two "include" statements at the very top. We covered those earlier in the book and now we will put them into play.

Include ('checkLogin.php') – Remember that?
Include ('config.php') – Remember that one too?

They are being put to use and both are "wrapped" with <?php and ?> because they are used by PHP.

The next section is for HTML. HTML pages have the structure shown below.

```
<html>
   <head>
      <meta tags><links><style>
   </head>
   <body>
      page structure
   </body>
</html>
```

GreenScape Granbury LLC

After you finish this book, a good place to purchase nice templates is on templatemonster.com. They have all types of ready-to-modify templates that will save you tons of time. You can embed PHP and MySQL into any of their HTML 5 types.

Let's go ahead and start the index.php page. Quick Note – An index file name can end with either .php or .html. If you are going to have PHP code inside the page, assign a .php domain type.

Create an index.php file in the /www directory where all your other files are. Copy the code below and paste it into the new file and save it.

Copy from "<?php" down to "?>" at the end of file. Not the first one you see.

```php
<?php

include ('checkLogin.php');
include ('config.php');

?>


<!DOCTYPE html>
<!-- Coding by CodingNepal | www.codingnepalweb.com -->
<html lang="en" dir="ltr">
  <head>
    <meta charset="UTF-8">
    <title> Responsiive Dashboard</title>
    <link rel="stylesheet" href="style.css">
    <!-- Boxicons CDN Link -->

    <meta name="viewport" content="width=device-width, initial-scale=1.0">
  </head>
<body>
 <div class="sidebar">
  <div class="logo-details">
```

```
  <i class='bx bxl-c-plus-plus'></i>
  <span class="logo_name">Greenscape</span>
</div>
 <ul class="nav-links">
  <li>
   <a href="index.php" class="active">
    <i class='bx bx-grid-alt' ></i>
    <span class="links_name">Dashboard</span>
   </a>
  </li>
  <li>
   <a href="insert.php">
    <i class='bx bx-box' ></i>
    <span class="links_name">Insert New Client</span>
   </a>
  </li>
  <li class="logout.php">
   <a href="logout.php">
    <i class='bx bx-cog'></i>
    <span class="links_name">Log out</span>
   </a>
  </li>
 </ul>
</div>
<section class="home-section">
 <nav>
  <div class="sidebar-button">
   <i class='bx bx-menu sidebarBtn'></i>
   <span class="dashboard">Dashboard</span>
  </div>
  <div class="search-box">
   <input type="text" placeholder="Search...">
   <i class='bx bx-search' ></i>
  </div>
  <div class="profile-details">
```

GreenScape Granbury LLC

```html
  <img src="images/profile.jpg" alt="">
  <span class="admin_name"><i>Greenscape</i></span>
  <i class='bx bx-chevron-down' ></i>
 </div>
</nav>
<div class="home-content">
 <div class="overview-boxes">
  <div class="box">
   <div class="right-side">
    <div class="box-topic">Total Order</div>
    <div class="number">40,876</div>
    <div class="indicator">
     <i class='bx bx-up-arrow-alt'></i>
     <span class="text">Up from yesterday</span>
    </div>
   </div>
   <i class='bx bx-cart-alt cart'></i>
  </div>
  <div class="box">
   <div class="right-side">
    <div class="box-topic">Total Sales</div>
    <div class="number">38,876</div>
    <div class="indicator">
     <i class='bx bx-up-arrow-alt'></i>
     <span class="text">Up from yesterday</span>
    </div>
   </div>
   <i class='bx bxs-cart-add cart two' ></i>
  </div>
  <div class="box">
   <div class="right-side">
    <div class="box-topic">Total Profit</div>
    <div class="number">$12,876</div>
    <div class="indicator">
     <i class='bx bx-up-arrow-alt'></i>
```

```html
        <span class="text">Up from yesterday</span>
      </div>
    </div>
    <i class='bx bx-cart cart three' ></i>
  </div>
  <div class="box">
   <div class="right-side">
    <div class="box-topic">Total Return</div>
    <div class="number">11,086</div>
    <div class="indicator">
     <i class='bx bx-down-arrow-alt down'></i>
     <span class="text">Down From Today</span>
    </div>
   </div>
   <i class='bx bxs-cart-download cart four' ></i>
  </div>
</div>
<div class="sales-boxes">
 <div class="recent-sales box">
  <div class="sales-details">

     <table width="100%" border="1" style="border-collapse:collapse;">
     <thead>
     <tr>
     <th><strong>S.No</strong></th>
     <th><strong>Last</strong></th>
     <th><strong>Email</strong></th>
     <th><strong>Edit</strong></th>
     <th><strong>Delete</strong></th>
     </tr>
     </thead>
     <tbody>

     <?php
      $count=1;
```

```php
            $sel_query="Select * from users ORDER BY uid desc;";
            $result = mysqli_query($db,$sel_query);
            while($row = mysqli_fetch_assoc($result)) { ?>
            <tr><td align="center"><?php echo $count; ?></td>
            <td align="center"><?php echo $row["last"]; ?></td>
            <td align="center"><?php echo $row["email"]; ?></td>
            <td align="center">
            <a href="edit.php?uid=<?php echo $row["uid"]; ?>">Edit</a>
            </td>
            <td align="center">
            <a href="delete.php?uid=<?php echo $row["uid"]; ?>">Delete</a>
            </td>
            </tr>
            <?php $count++; } ?>
            </tbody>
            </table>
            </div>
    </div>
    </div>
  </div>
 </div>
 </section>
 <script>
  let sidebar = document.querySelector(".sidebar");
let sidebarBtn = document.querySelector(".sidebarBtn");
sidebarBtn.onclick = function() {
 sidebar.classList.toggle("active");
 if(sidebar.classList.contains("active")){
 sidebarBtn.classList.replace("bx-menu" ,"bx-menu-alt-right");
} else {
 sidebarBtn.classList.replace("bx-menu-alt-right", "bx-menu");
}
 </script>
</body>
</html>
```

GreenScape Granbury LLC

Now, let's test the index.php file. Start your browser and type in "localhost". By default, the system runs index.php or index.html. We don't have an index.html so it runs index.php.

When index.php is executed, it hits the "include ('checkLogin.php') "statement which checks whether you are logged in or not. If not, you are directed to login.php where you are prompted to login.

Hopefully, you will be on the login.php page. If so, enter you login id and password that you created under "Seeding the Database".

If your login works, you should be directed to the index.php file.

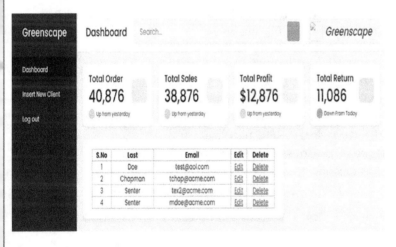

GreenScape Granbury LLC

Let's Finish Up

Since the index.php file is now up, we need to add a few more PHP applications. See the listing below for the name and purpose.

1. Delete.php: This file is for deleting existing clients.
2. Edit.php: This file is for editing existing clients.
3. Logout.php: This file is for logging out of the application.
4. Register.php: This file allows a new client to register themselves.
5. Insert.php: This file is for adding new clients by the staff.

Most of these files are short in length. We will start with Logout.php and work our way backwards. As you have done in other sections of this book, you are going to copy and paste the code below.

1. Create a new file called **delete.php** in the /www directory. Copy the following code and paste it into the new file and save it.

```php
<?php
require('checkLogin.php');
require('config.php');
$uid=$_REQUEST['uid'];
$query = "DELETE FROM users WHERE uid=$uid";
$result = mysqli_query($db,$query) or die ( mysqli_error($db));
header("Location: index.php");
exit();
?>
```

2. Create a new file called **edit.php** in the /www directory. Copy the following code and paste it into the new file and save it.

```php
<?php

include ('checkLogin.php');
include ('config.php');

$uid=$_REQUEST['uid'];
$query = "SELECT * FROM users WHERE uid='".$uid."'";
$result = mysqli_query($db, $query) or die ( mysqli_error($db));
$row = mysqli_fetch_assoc($result);

?>

<!DOCTYPE html>
<!-- Coding by CodingNepal | www.codingnepalweb.com -->
<html lang="en" dir="ltr">
  <head>
    <meta charset="UTF-8">
    <title>Update Client</title>
    <link rel="stylesheet" href="style.css">
    <!-- Boxicons CDN Link -->

    <meta name="viewport" content="width=device-width, initial-scale=1.0">
  </head>
<body>
  <div class="sidebar">
   <div class="logo-details">
    <i class='bx bxl-c-plus-plus'></i>
    <span class="logo_name">Greenscape</span>
   </div>
    <ul class="nav-links">
      <li>
```

```
        <a href="index.php" class="active">
         <i class='bx bx-grid-alt' ></i>
         <span class="links_name">Dashboard</span>
        </a>
       </li>
       <li>
        <a href="insert.php">
         <i class='bx bx-box' ></i>
         <span class="links_name">Insert New Client</span>
        </a>
       </li>
       <li>
        <a href="index.php">
         <i class='bx bx-list-ul' ></i>
         <span class="links_name">List Clients</span>
        </a>
       </li>
       <li class="logout.php">
        <a href="logout.php">
         <i class='bx bx-cog'></i>
         <span class="links_name">Log out</span>
        </a>
       </li>
      </ul>
     </div>
     <section class="home-section">
      <nav>
       <div class="sidebar-button">
        <i class='bx bx-menu sidebarBtn'></i>
        <span class="dashboard">Dashboard</span>
       </div>
       <div class="search-box">
        <input type="text" placeholder="Search...">
        <i class='bx bx-search' ></i>
       </div>
       <div class="profile-details">
        <img src="images/profile.jpg" alt="">
        <span class="admin_name"><i>Greenscape</i></span>
```

```
      <i class='bx bx-chevron-down' ></i>
    </div>
  </nav>
  <div class="home-content">
    <div class="overview-boxes">
      <div class="box">
        <div class="right-side">
          <div class="box-topic">Total Order</div>
          <div class="number">40,876</div>
          <div class="indicator">
            <i class='bx bx-up-arrow-alt'></i>
            <span class="text">Up from yesterday</span>
          </div>
        </div>
        <i class='bx bx-cart-alt cart'></i>
      </div>
      <div class="box">
        <div class="right-side">
          <div class="box-topic">Total Sales</div>
          <div class="number">38,876</div>
          <div class="indicator">
            <i class='bx bx-up-arrow-alt'></i>
            <span class="text">Up from yesterday</span>
          </div>
        </div>
        <i class='bx bxs-cart-add cart two' ></i>
      </div>
      <div class="box">
        <div class="right-side">
          <div class="box-topic">Total Profit</div>
          <div class="number">$12,876</div>
          <div class="indicator">
            <i class='bx bx-up-arrow-alt'></i>
            <span class="text">Up from yesterday</span>
          </div>
        </div>
        <i class='bx bx-cart cart three' ></i>
      </div>
```

GreenScape Granbury LLC

```html
<div class="box">
  <div class="right-side">
    <div class="box-topic">Total Return</div>
    <div class="number">11,086</div>
    <div class="indicator">
      <i class='bx bx-down-arrow-alt down'></i>
      <span class="text">Down From Today</span>
    </div>
  </div>
  <i class='bx bxs-cart-download cart four' ></i>
  </div>
</div>
<div class="sales-boxes">
  <div class="recent-sales box">

    <div class="sales-details">

      <div class="form">

      <div>
      <h1>Update Client</h1>
```
```php
<?php
$status = "";
if(isset($_POST['new']) && $_POST['new']==1)
{
$uid=$_REQUEST['uid'];
$first =$_REQUEST['first'];
$last =$_REQUEST['last'];
$email =$_REQUEST['email'];
$username =$_REQUEST['username'];
$password =$_REQUEST['password'];

$update="UPDATE users SET first='".$first."',
last='".$last."', email='".$email."',
password='".$password."' where uid='".$uid."'";
mysqli_query($db, $update) or die(mysqli_error($db));
$status = "Record Updated Successfully. </br></br>
```

GreenScape Granbury LLC

```
            <a href='index.php'>View Updated Record</a>";
            echo '<p style="color:#FF0000;">'.$status.'</p>';
            } else {
            ?>

            <form name="form" method="post" action="">
            <input type="hidden" name="new" value="1" />
            <input name="uid" type="hidden" value="<?php echo $row['uid'];?>" />

            <p><br /><input type="text" name="first"
              value="<?php echo $row['first'];?>" /> First Name</p>
            <p><br /><input type="text" name="last"
              value="<?php echo $row['last'];?>" /> Last Name</p>
            <p><br /><input type="text" name="email"
              value="<?php echo $row['email'];?>" /> Email Address</p>
            <p><br /><input type="text" name="username"
              value="<?php echo $row['username'];?>" /> User ID</p>
             <p><br /><input type="text" name="password"
                value="<?php echo $row['password'];?>" /> Password</p>

            <p><br /><input name="submit" type="submit" value="Update" /></p>
            </form>
            <?php } ?>
            </div>
            </div>

        </div>

      </div>

    </div>
    </div>
    </section>
    <script>
    let sidebar = document.querySelector(".sidebar");
    let sidebarBtn = document.querySelector(".sidebarBtn");
    sidebarBtn.onclick = function() {
     sidebar.classList.toggle("active");
```

```
    if(sidebar.classList.contains("active")){
    sidebarBtn.classList.replace("bx-menu" ,"bx-menu-alt-right");
    }else
    sidebarBtn.classList.replace("bx-menu-alt-right", "bx-menu");
    }
   </script>
   </body>
   </html>
```

3. Create a new file called **logout.php** in the /www directory. Copy the following code and paste it into the new file and save it.

```php
<?php
//start the session
session_start();

//check to make sure the session variable is registered
if (!isset($_SESSION[$user])) {

//session variable is registered, the user is ready to logout
session_unset();
session_destroy();
header( "Location: login.php" );
}
else{

//the session variable isn't registered, the user shouldn't even be on this page
header( "Location: login.php" );
}
?>
```

4. Create a new file called **register.php** in the /www directory. Copy the following code and paste it into the new file and save it.

GreenScape Granbury LLC

```php
<?php
session_start();

include ('config.php');
error_reporting(E_ALL);
ini_set("display_errors", 1);

//Check if the form is submitted
if (isset ($_POST['submit'])) {

    $problem = FALSE;

    //Check each value submitted
    if (empty ($_POST['username'])) {
        $problem = TRUE;
        print '<p>Please enter a user id.</p>';
    } else {
        $username = $_POST['username'];
    }

    if (empty ($_POST['first'])) {
        $problem = TRUE;
        print '<p>Please enter your first name.</p>';
    } else {
        $first = $_POST['first'];
    }

    if (empty ($_POST['last'])) {
        $problem = TRUE;
        print '<p>Please enter your last name.</p>';
    } else {
        $last = $_POST['last'];
    }

    if (empty ($_POST['email'])) {
        $problem = TRUE;
        print '<p>Please enter your email address.</p>';
    } else {
```

```php
      $email = $_POST['email'];
   }

   if (empty ($_POST['password'])) {
     $problem = TRUE;
     print '<p>Please enter your password.</p>';
   }

   if (empty ($_POST['password2'])) {
     $problem = TRUE;
     print '<p>Please confirm your password.</p>';
   }

   if ($_POST['password'] != $_POST['password2']) {
     $problem = TRUE;
     print '<p>Your passwords did not match!</p>';
   } else {
     $password = $_POST['password'];
   }

   if (!$problem) { //No problems

   //Write the registration data to the users table
   @$sql=mysqli_query($db,"INSERT INTO users (username, first, last, email,
password)
   VALUES ('$username', '$first', '$last', '$email', '$password')");

   if (!$sql) {
   print "<p>Could not add the record because: <b>" . mysqli_error() .
   "</b> . The query was $sql . </p><br />" . '<a href="register.php">Click Here to
Return</a></div>';
   } else {
     print '<p>Registration Successful</p>';
   }
  }    //End of no problem
 }
 ?>
```

```
<!DOCTYPE html>
<html lang="en">
 <head>
  <meta charset="UTF-8">
  <meta name="viewport" content="width=device-width, initial-scale=1.0">
  <title>Registration or Sign Up</title>
  <link rel="stylesheet" href="stylelr.css">
 </head>
<body>
 <div class="wrapper">
  <h2>Registration</h2>
  <form action="<?php echo $_SERVER['PHP_SELF']; ?>" method="post">
   <div class="input-box">
    <input type="text" name="username" placeholder="Enter your username"
required>
   </div>
   <div class="input-box">
    <input type="text" name="email" placeholder="Enter your email" required>
   </div>
   <div class="input-box">
    <input type="text" name="first" placeholder="Enter your first name" required>
   </div>
   <div class="input-box">
    <input type="text" name="last" placeholder="Enter your last name" required>
   </div>
   <div class="input-box">
    <input type="password" name="password" placeholder="Create password"
required>
   </div>
   <div class="input-box">
    <input type="password" name="password2" placeholder="Confirm password"
required>
   </div>
   <div class="policy">
    <input type="checkbox">
    <h3>I accept all terms & condition</h3>
   </div>
   <div class="input-box button">
```

GreenScape Granbury LLC

```
      <input type="Submit" name="submit" value="Register Now">
      </div>
      <div class="text">
       <h3>Already have an account? <a href="login.php">Login now</a></h3>
      </div>
     </form>
    </div>
   </body>
  </html>
```

5. Create a new file called **insert.php** in the /www directory. Copy the following code and paste it into the new file and save it.

```php
<?php

include ('checkLogin.php');
include ('config.php');

$status = "";
if(isset($_POST['new']) && $_POST['new']==1){

   $first =$_REQUEST['first'];
   $last = $_REQUEST['last'];
   $email = $_REQUEST['email'];
   $username = $_REQUEST['username'];
   $password = $_REQUEST['password'];

   $ins_query="INSERT INTO users (username, first, last, email, password)
      VALUES ('$username', '$first', '$last', '$email', '$password')";

   mysqli_query($db,$ins_query)
   or die(mysqli_error($db));
   $status = "New Record Inserted Successfully.
   </br></br><a href='index2.php'>View Inserted Record</a>";
}
```

```
    ?>


    <!DOCTYPE html>
    <!-- Coding by CodingNepal | www.codingnepalweb.com -->
    <html lang="en" dir="ltr">
     <head>
      <meta charset="UTF-8">
      <title>Insert New Client</title>
      <link rel="stylesheet" href="style.css">
      <!-- Boxicons CDN Link -->

       <meta name="viewport" content="width=device-width, initial-scale=1.0">
      </head>
    <body>
     <div class="sidebar">
      <div class="logo-details">
       <i class='bx bxl-c-plus-plus'></i>
       <span class="logo_name">Greenscape</span>
      </div>
       <ul class="nav-links">
        <li>
         <a href="index.php" class="active">
          <i class='bx bx-grid-alt' ></i>
          <span class="links_name">Dashboard</span>
         </a>
        </li>
        <li>
         <a href="index.php">
          <i class='bx bx-list-ul' ></i>
          <span class="links_name">List Clients</span>
         </a>
        </li>
        <li>
         <a href="insert.php">
          <i class='bx bx-box' ></i>
          <span class="links_name">Insert New Client</span>
         </a>
```

```html
        </li>
        <li class="logout.php">
         <a href="logout.php">
          <i class='bx bx-cog'></i>
          <span class="links_name">Log out</span>
         </a>
        </li>
       </ul>
      </div>
      <section class="home-section">
       <nav>
        <div class="sidebar-button">
         <i class='bx bx-menu sidebarBtn'></i>
         <span class="dashboard">Dashboard</span>
        </div>
        <div class="search-box">
         <input type="text" placeholder="Search...">
         <i class='bx bx-search' ></i>
        </div>
        <div class="profile-details">
         <img src="images/profile.jpg" alt="">
         <span class="admin_name"><i>Greenscape</i></span>
         <i class='bx bx-chevron-down' ></i>
        </div>
       </nav>
       <div class="home-content">
        <div class="overview-boxes">
         <div class="box">
          <div class="right-side">
           <div class="box-topic">Total Order</div>
           <div class="number">40,876</div>
           <div class="indicator">
            <i class='bx bx-up-arrow-alt'></i>
            <span class="text">Up from yesterday</span>
           </div>
          </div>
          <i class='bx bx-cart-alt cart'></i>
         </div>
```

```
<div class="box">
 <div class="right-side">
  <div class="box-topic">Total Sales</div>
  <div class="number">38,876</div>
  <div class="indicator">
   <i class='bx bx-up-arrow-alt'></i>
   <span class="text">Up from yesterday</span>
  </div>
 </div>
 <i class='bx bxs-cart-add cart two' ></i>
</div>
<div class="box">
 <div class="right-side">
  <div class="box-topic">Total Profit</div>
  <div class="number">$12,876</div>
  <div class="indicator">
   <i class='bx bx-up-arrow-alt'></i>
   <span class="text">Up from yesterday</span>
  </div>
 </div>
 <i class='bx bx-cart cart three' ></i>
</div>
<div class="box">
 <div class="right-side">
  <div class="box-topic">Total Return</div>
  <div class="number">11,086</div>
  <div class="indicator">
   <i class='bx bx-down-arrow-alt down'></i>
   <span class="text">Down From Today</span>
  </div>
 </div>
 <i class='bx bxs-cart-download cart four' ></i>
</div>
</div>
<div class="sales-boxes">
 <div class="recent-sales box">
  <div class="sales-details">
   <div class="form">
```

```
<div>
<h1>Add New Client</h1>
<form name="form" method="post" action="">
<input type="hidden" name="new" value="1" />

<p><br /><input type="text" name="first" placeholder="Enter First Name"
required /></p>
<p><br /><input type="text" name="last" placeholder="Enter Last Name"
required /></p>
<p><br /><input type="text" name="email" placeholder="Enter Email
Address" required /></p>
<p><br /><input type="text" name="username" placeholder="Enter User
Name" required /></p>
<p><br /><input type="password" name="password" placeholder="Enter Your
password" required /></p>
<p><br /><input name="submit" type="submit" value="Submit" /></p>
</form>
<p style="color:#FF0000;"><?php echo $status; ?></p>
</div>
</div>
</div>
</div>
</div>
</div>
</section>
<script>
let sidebar = document.querySelector(".sidebar");
let sidebarBtn = document.querySelector(".sidebarBtn");
sidebarBtn.onclick = function() {
sidebar.classList.toggle("active");
if(sidebar.classList.contains("active")){
sidebarBtn.classList.replace("bx-menu" ,"bx-menu-alt-right");
} else {
sidebarBtn.classList.replace("bx-menu-alt-right", "bx-menu");
}
</script>
</body>
</html>
```

GreenScape Granbury LLC

Testing Your New Website

Now that all your code has been built, you are ready to test and make sure everything is working as intended.

Start with the Login page. If you start your browser and enter "localhost", you should be taken to the login page. Enter your credentials and you will be forwarded to Index.php or the home page.

It will look like the image from a few pages back.

The Layout of the Dashboard.

I have posted the image of the dashboard again for your reference.

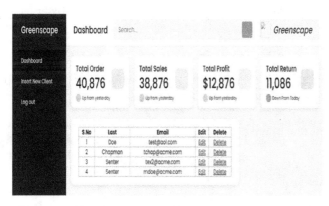

Tip: Run "Insert New Client". Add some bogus information in each field to create a new client. Add several as shown in the image above. Make sure this works. When you save each record, you will be directed back to the Dashboard.

Next, click "Delete" next to the record you wish to remove. Insure this removes the record you wish to delete.

Next, test "Edit" to the right of each record. This calls the edit.php file for editing the record on the same line. It is actually the same application you used in the menu bar in the far-left column.

Now, test the "Log Out" link in the left column. It should logout and return you to the login panel. While on the login panel, click the registration on the bottom of the box. Make sure it works. Go through the registration panel, complete each field, and save. Then login and ensure the record you just entered shows up on the Dashboard.

Summary

Now that your website is working, what do you do with it? If you wish to use this website on the internet, I suggest that you look at another one of my eBooks or paperbacks. I am referring to "How to Build Your Own Web Server by Wesley Senter", listed on Amazon.

It will step you through building a web server that is panel driven by CWP. The alternative is to lease a VPS. A domain name is required along with a public IP address for the server and your domain name registrar.

The book explains all of this.

A Note About this Book

I have helped you build a working website using HTML, PHP, CSS, and MySQL. I hope you have enjoyed the experience. To learn all these programming languages up-close, I would suggest you buy some books. One for each language.

You can go through each file and pick it apart using Google to learn the details. Then, write variations of what I included. It will take you some time, but once you learn how all four of these languages fit together, you will be able to write your own.

Thank you so much for purchasing my eBook.

GreenScape Granbury LLC

Wes Senter

** If you are absolutely stuck, email me and I will help.

Email: wes@greenscapellc.com

About the Author

The author of "How to Build Your Own Home Recording Studio" is Wes Senter. Wes is a Computer Scientist, trained as a Network Engineer by the U.S. Air Force. He has over thirty-five years of experience in Information Technology. He is both Cisco and Microsoft Certified (CCNA, MCSE). His fields of expertise are listed below.

Today, Wes owns a book publishing company, "Greenscape Granbury LLC" and writes different types of books for publication. He is also a songwriter, music producer, and music publisher. He has released three albums and two singles which can be heard on any streaming service such as Spotify and Pandora.

- Network Engineering
- Network Management
- Network Architecture
- Applications Design
- Applications Authoring
- Web Design
- Web Programming
- IBM Systems Programming
- IBM SNAP/D
- Technical Documentation
- Technical Diagramming
- eBook Authoring
- Paperback Authoring
- Music Producer
- Country Music Artist
- Songwriter
- Runs a Recording Studio

References

Peachpit Press (2004); PHP for the World Wide Web. 1249 Eighth St., Berkley, CA 94710

Greenscape Granbury LLC (2023). *How To Build a Website with HTML, CSS, PHP, and MySQL.* 3724 Cove Timber Ave. Granbury, TX 76049

www.ingramcontent.com/pod-product-compliance
Lightning Source LLC
LaVergne TN
LVHW051614050326
832903LV00033B/4502